Teaching Tips

Encouraging Topic Interest

Help students to develop an understanding of and appreciation for different health concepts. Engage students through stories, non-fiction books, videos, posters, and other resources as a springboard for learning.

Black Line Masters and Graphic Organizers

Encourage students to use the black line masters and graphic organizers to present information and reinforce important concepts, and to extend opportunities for learning. The graphic organizers will help students focus on important ideas or make direct comparisons.

Learning Logs

Keeping a learning log is an effective way for students to organize their thoughts and ideas about the health concepts presented. Student learning logs also give the teacher insight onto which follow-up activities are needed to review and clarify concepts learned.

Learning logs can include the following kinds of entries:

- Teacher prompts
- Student personal reflections
- Questions that arise
- Connections discovered
- Labeled diagrams and pictures

Culminating Activity: Create a Health Magazine

Have students demonstrate what they have learned about health by creating a kids' health magazine. This culminating activity can be done as a class project, in small groups, or independently. Encourage students to browse through magazines to get ideas. Student checklists are included.

Rubrics and Checklists

Use the rubrics and checklists in this book to assess student learning.

Table of Contents

All About Me: Activity Ideas

Activity Idea: Websites About Growing Up

Puberty is the transitional time between childhood and adulthood. The changes that occur during puberty do not follow a strict timeline. Puberty is unique for each child. This can be a very difficult and confusing time for children. Here are some excellent websites about growing up and the stages of puberty:

http://www.childdevelopmentinfo.com/development/puberty.htm

This website gives excellent information for parents on how to share information with their child.

http://www.kidshealth.org/kid/grow/body_stuff/puberty.html

Encourage students to learn more about what might be or will be happening to their bodies. This website is written in kid-friendly language and has abundant information.

Extension:

- Introduce a question box where students can ask questions anonymously.
- Discuss with students the benefits, opportunities, challenges, and responsibilities of growing up.

Activity Idea: My Strengths and Weaknesses

Have students complete a web graphic organizer to show their strengths, and another web to show things they think they need to improve on. Reinforce the idea that everyone has strengths and weaknesses.

Discussion Starters:

- How do you feel when you do something well?
- Do you think it is okay to have things to improve on?
- Pick one thing you would like to improve. What are the steps you need to take to do this?

Activity Idea: The People in Your Life

Encourage students to think about the people in their life. Have students think about how people are close to them for different reasons.

Discussion Starters:

- Who are the most important people in your life? Why?
- Who are the people that make you feel special or important?
- Whom can you go to if you have a problem?
- Do you think it is important to let your family know if you are feeling upset, angry, or anxious about something? Explain your thinking.
- Would you speak to a friend the same way you would speak to your parent(s)? Why?

Activity Idea: Dealing with Peer Pressure

As a whole group, discuss peer pressure — pressure from people your own age to do things you normally wouldn't do on your own. Peer pressure can be both positive and negative. Create a class T-chart and list examples of both positive and negative peer pressure.

Discussion Starters:

- Why do you think people like to belong to a group?
- What does it take to stand up to negative peer pressure?
- Have you ever experienced negative peer pressure where you almost did or did do something you did not want to do? If so, what happened, and how did it make you feel?
- Have you ever experienced positive peer pressure that led you to try something new? If so, what happened, and how did it make you feel?

Introducing...

Create a collage using pictures, words, or symbols clipped from magazines that represent things about you, things you enjoy doing, places you have visited, people you admire, and things you like about yourself.

One of the things I like about myself is...

Student Interview

Interview a fellow student in the class.

Student Interview

Name ____

Date of Birth _______________________ **Grade** ___________

a. List three words to describe you.

b. What is your favorite color?

c. What is your favorite food?

d. What is your favorite movie?

e. What is your favorite book?

f. What is your favorite activity outside school?

g. Which activity do you dislike?

h. Name a person you admire a lot. Tell why.

i. What do you want to be when you grow up?

j. What place would you like to visit someday?

A Timeline

Create a timeline to show the important events in your life.

Age	Important Event
1.	
2.	
3.	
4.	
5.	
6.	
7.	
8.	

Changes or Milestones in Your Life

In the chart below, identify a change or a milestone in your life. An example might be moving to another place or getting a new pet.

1. What was a change in your life?

2. What happened after the change?

3. How did you feel about the change?

Circle of the People in Your Life

Think about the people in your life. Put your name in the center circle. Next, place names of immediate family members, relatives, friends, and other people in your life in the circles around you. If you feel close to a person, write their name in a circle nearest to you. As you feel less close to a person, write their name in a circle farther away from you.

Brain Stretch:

a) Look at your circle of people. Why did you make some of your choices?

____

____

b) Do you think your circle of people could ever change? Explain.

____

____

Getting Along with Others

People get along better when they cooperate and listen to each other.
Take the survey and think about how well you get along with others.

Cooperation Skills	Always	Sometimes	Never
1. I share with others.			
2. I take turns.			
3. I take responsibility for my share of group work.			
4. I give compliments when someone is doing well.			
5. I talk about disagreements and problem-solve.			
6. I invite people to join a group.			

Listening Skills	Always	Sometimes	Never
1. I listen to others without interrupting.			
2. I concentrate on what the speaker is saying.			
3. I ask questions to ensure understanding or to find out more.			
4. I look at the person while they are speaking.			
5. I can accurately repeat what someone has said.			

Listening Skills	Always	Sometimes	Never
1. I speak clearly.			
2. I look at the person I am speaking to.			
3. I speak loud enough that people can hear me.			

Brain Stretch: Getting Along with Others

1. Review your responses. How would you rate your "getting along with others" skills? Explain.

____

____

____

____

2. In what way do you need to improve?

____

____

____

____

3. How do you think you can use these skills in everyday life?

____

____

____

____

4. Why do you think it is easier to get along with some people and not others?

____

____

____

____

Family Members Work Together

Think about your role in your family. How do you contribute? How do you help? Complete the chart below to show how each family member contributes to help everyone work together.

Family Member	Job or Contribution

Brain Stretch:

What would happen if your family did not work together? Explain.

Likenesses and Differences

Everyone has likenesses and differences. Find someone in your class who:

• has the same favorite color as you	• is taller than you	• was born in another town or city	• has a different birthday month than you
• likes to do art activities	• has the same color eyes	• takes some kind of lessons	• has a pet
• has the same birthday month as you	• doesn't have a pet	• plays an instrument	• can speak another language
• is shorter than you	• likes vegetables	• is wearing blue jeans	• is the same height

Be an Advice Columnist

Pretend you are the advice columnist for a kids' health magazine. Read the following letters and write a letter of advice for each.

Dear Adviser,

My friends have told me that I have to steal something in order to be in their special group. If I don't do it, they say they won't be my friends.

I want them to be my friends, but I don't want to steal!

What should I do?

Dear Adviser,

My friend wants me to try out for the school soccer team with her.

I really like to play soccer, but I don't want to embarrass myself.

What should I do?

Dear Adviser,

All my friends have already kissed somebody. I feel like I am the only one left who hasn't. I don't feel like I belong around my friends. All they do is talk about kissing.

Should I just kiss someone to get it over with?

What should I do?

Dear Adviser,

I really want to be in the school choir. My friends say I have a great voice and should try out. My friends said they would come with me and try out too.

I still feel nervous.

What should I do?

Dear Adviser,

I am really good at math and we have a test soon. My friend wants to cheat off me. He says that if I am his real friend I will let him.

I don't think that is right.

What should I do?

Dear Adviser,

I am in a new class this year. My new friends in my class don't like my best friend. They say I have to choose between my best friend and them.

What should I do?

Just Say "NO"

Here are some tips on how to say "NO!" if you find yourself in an uncomfortable situation with a friend or group of people.

Tip 1

Remember always to look the person straight in the eye, and to firmly state your position. For example:

No, I won't do that, that's illegal!

No, I won't do that, that's dangerous!

No, I won't do that, it could make me sick!

No, I don't want to.

Tip 2

Suggest an alternative activity or place to go. This will make it easier for others to go along with you. For example:

Let's go to my house instead.

Let's go to the park.

Tip 3

If you can't change your friend's mind, walk away, but let your friend know it is their choice whether to join you or not. For example:

Well, I'm leaving. If you change your mind, come join me at ___________________.

Make a list of situations where you would say "NO!"

1. _______________________

2. _______________________

3. _______________________

4. _______________________

5. _______________________

6. _______________________

7. _______________________

8. _______________________

Healthy Habits: Activity Ideas

Activity Idea: Having a Healthy Lifestyle

It is important to encourage students to form healthy habits from a young age. In a whole group, review the concept of a healthy lifestyle. A healthy lifestyle involves four parts: healthy eating, regular exercise, enough sleep and time to relax. List the four parts on chart paper and have students brainstorm and list things they can do to support each part.

Extension:

- Invite guest speakers from various organizations to talk to students about how they can have a healthy lifestyle.

Activity Idea: Kids' Health Website

The website below is an excellent way for students to learn more about healthy habits. There is abundant information available in kid-friendly language. There are also many games and other interactive activities where students can find out about: Dealing with Feelings; Staying Healthy; People, Places, and Things That Help Me; and Growing Up.

http://kidshealth.org/kids/

Activity Idea: Dealing With Stress

Students have to deal with stress, just as adults do. Many children have the responsibility not only of schoolwork, but of extracurricular activities, family chores, or other obligations. With so many activities on the go, children might not have the opportunity to relax and take time for themselves. As a result, students may be tired, overwhelmed, and worried if they don't complete everything they need to. Use a web graphic organizer to brainstorm ideas for dealing with stress and worries. For example: listening to music, exercising, making a schedule with a list they can check off as they complete things, or getting enough sleep.

Discussion Starters:

- What does the term "stressed" mean?
- How does it feel to be stressed?
- Do you ever worry about things? If so, what are some examples?
- Whom can you go to if you are worried about something?

Activity Idea: The Five Food Groups

Introduce students to the idea that food can be classified into five food groups. Tell them about MyPlate Food Guide, and how there are recommended amounts from each food group that kids should eat each day. Different foods give our bodies important nutrients. Carbohydrates such as potatoes, bread, and cereal give energy. Proteins in meats, fish, nuts, eggs, and some plants help make our bodies grow strong. Vitamins and minerals in fruit, milk products, and vegetables help our bones, teeth, and skin stay healthy. Water helps carry all other nutrients to different areas in the body.

On chart paper post the headings of the five food groups: fruits, vegetables, grains, protein, and dairy. Have the students brainstorm food items and record them under the appropriate food group heading.

Encourage students to visit the website below and play Nutrition Café. These games offer students the opportunity to test their food knowledge.

http://www.nourishinteractive.com/kids/healthy-games

Activity Idea: Calories Are Units of Energy

Introduce to students the idea that a calorie is a unit of energy that comes from the food we eat. Some foods, such as sugary treats, have lots of calories. Other foods, such as celery, have very few calories. Reinforce the idea that calories aren't bad for you and that your body needs calories for energy. It is only when you eat too many calories and do not burn enough energy through activity that calories can lead to weight gain.

The recommended range of calories for most school-age children is 1,600 to 2,500 per day. Keep in mind that each person's body burns energy, or calories, at different rates depending on their size and level of physical activity. Consequently, there is not one fixed number of calories that each child should eat.

Healthy Habits: Activity Ideas (continued)

Activity Idea: Examining Nutritional Values on Packaging

Have students collect and bring in empty cereal boxes, juice boxes, or other food packages. After giving some background information on nutrients, ask students in a small-group setting to examine the nutritional level of various brands. The teacher may wish to have different groups responsible for different types of food items, including: cereal, juice boxes, snacks, etc. Next, have groups report on which items had the best nutritional value compared with similar products.

Discussion Starters:

- . After learning about the importance of nutritional information, would you change your buying habits?
- What surprised you?
- How did the packaging entice consumers?
- What are the characteristics of a smart consumer?

Activity Idea: Compare Nutritional Values

Ask students to bring a juice box or label from a juice container to class.

1. Ask students how pure they think their juice is just by looking at the package.
   For example, the packaging may feature pictures of fruit, or phrases such as "made with pure juice."
2. Next, ask the students to look at the ingredients.
3. Ask students for the first two main ingredients. What are they?
4. Does their juice have pure juice as one of the main ingredients?
5. Does their juice have water and sugar and/or glucose-fructose as the two main ingredients?
6. What other ingredients are in their juices?
7. Would they recommend their juice as a healthy drink choice? Why or why not?
8. Rate the brands of fruit juices from the most healthy to the least healthy.

Repeat the above activity using snack-food packaging.

Activity Idea: Be Consumer Savvy

Introduce students to the ways of being consumer savvy, particularly the ways in which packaging is designed to attract kids. Brainstorm with the class how advertisers use the design, promotion, and marketing of products to sell to consumers. Have students compare similar food products using a T-chart and assess the nutritional value of the foods and beverages they enjoy.

Discussion Starters:

- Why do you think manufacturers feature famous people or cartoon characters on the front of a package? Explain your thinking.
- Do you think gimmicks such as contests, recipes, or free gifts help entice consumers to buy a product?
- Have you ever noticed how sometimes the amount of a product, in relation to the size of the package, is off? For instance, a small amount of candies is put in a big bag. Why would manufacturers do that?

Activity Idea: Create a Class Cookbook

Ask students to bring in their favorite healthy recipes and combine them to make a class cookbook.

Activity Idea: Create a Commercial

Using the commercial black line master as a guide, have students create and perform a commercial for a healthy food item.

Healthy Eating: Journal Topics

1. Why do you think it is important to have a balanced diet?

2. How do you think what you eat affects your body and the way you feel?

3. Do you think the media influence your eating habits? Explain your thinking.

4. What do you think the difference is between a snack and a treat?

5. Do your eating habits change from when you are at home to when you are with your friends or out at a restaurant? Explain.

6. What can you do to maintain a healthy body weight?

7. Do you like to eat breakfast? Why or why not?

8. Name some of your favorite foods. Why are they your favorite?

9. Are there any foods you refuse to eat? Explain.

10. Do you check the nutritional information of the food items you eat? Why or why not?

11. Do you think convenience foods (frozen foods, canned foods, fast food) make it easier or harder to have a healthy diet? Explain your thinking.

MyPlate Food Guide

Vegetables
40% of your plate

salad

juice

Fruits
10% of your plate

Grains
30% of your plate

cereal

bread

rice

pasta

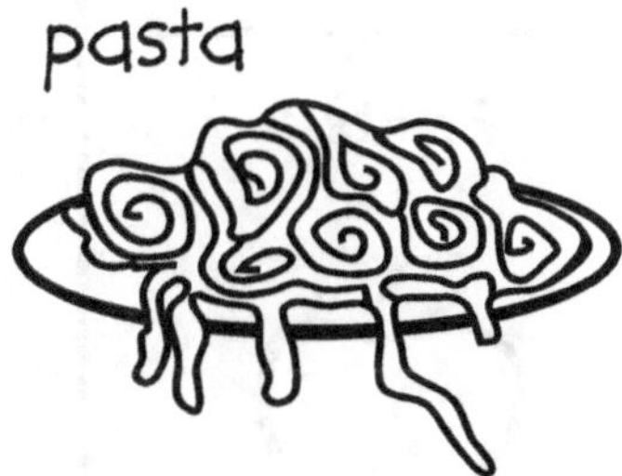

Dairy
1 cup of milk, yogurt, or soy milk, 1½ ounces of natural cheese, or 2 ounces of processed cheese

milk

cheese

yogurt

Protein
20% of your plate

egg

peanut
butter

poultry

beans

meat

fish

The Five Food Groups and You

List the kinds of foods you like to eat in each of the five food groups.

1. Grains

For example, bread, pasta, rice, tortilla, popcorn, matzo

2. Vegetables

For example, green beans, carrots, spinach, red pepper, eggplant, kale

3. Fruits

For example, orange, kiwi, apple, papaya, pear, mango, cherry, blueberry

4. Dairy

For example, milk, yogurt, cheese

4. Protein

For example, eggs, nuts, seeds, fish, poultry, meat, beans, tofu, tempeh

What is your favorite food group? ___________________________

A Healthy Eating Survey

Complete the survey to learn more about your eating habits.

	Questions	Rarely	Sometimes	Often
1.	Do you eat three balanced meals a day?			
2.	Do you eat healthy snacks?			
3.	Do you eat breakfast?			
4.	Do you eat lots of high-calorie treats?			
5.	Do you eat late at night?			
6.	Do you drink at least a few glasses of water every day?			
7.	Do you eat regularly at a restaurant?			
8.	Do you eat a lot of junk food or fast food?			
9.	Do you eat when you are stressed, or upset?			
10.	Do you eat from each food group every day?			

Using this survey as a guide, comment on your eating habits. How could your eating habits improve?

Create Packaging for a New Cereal

Take an empty cereal box and create new packaging for an imaginary cereal. Make sure to include:

- nutritional guide
- price
- picture
- enticing slogan

Use the space below to help plan your cereal box.

Fast Food Know-How

Pretend you are going to a fast-food restaurant.

1. Fill out the menu order form according to what you would like to eat. Try to be realistic.
2. Next, look up on the restaurant's nutritional guide the calories and and grams of fat for each item you ordered, and record.
3. Add up the numbers to find out the total calories and grams of fat you would eat by having your meal.
4. Try to plan a more nutritious meal at this fast-food restaurant.

1. **Name of the restaurant:**

Menu Item	Calories	Grams of Fat
Total:		

2. **Name of the restaurant:**

Menu Item	Calories	Grams of Fat
Total:		

Brain Stretch: Fast Food Know-How

1. What surprised you?

____

____

____

2. How do you think your ordering habits might change?

____

____

____

3. Do you think most people realize how many calories and grams of fat they are really eating? Explain your thinking.

____

____

____

4. List some suggestions you would give to your favorite fast-food restaurant to make their menu more healthy.

____

____

____

Healthy Food Collage

Cut and paste pictures of healthy food from flyers or magazines.
to create a collage. Try to include pictures from all the food groups.

Write about your healthy food collage:

____

____

Eat Healthy Poster

Create a poster with a message to encourage people to Eat Healthy!
Make sure your poster includes a message and a picture.

Plan a Healthy Eating Day

List the different kinds of foods and the portion sizes you would eat in a day.

1.	**Breakfast**	
2.	**Healthy Snack**	
3.	**Lunch**	
4.	**Healthy Snack**	
5.	**Dinner**	
6.	**What are some healthy drink choices?**	

How many portions of each food group did you include in your plan?

Grains: ☐☐☐☐☐☐☐   Fruits: ☐☐☐☐☐☐☐   Dairy: ☐☐☐☐☐☐☐

Vegetables: ☐☐☐☐☐☐☐   Protein: ☐☐☐☐☐☐☐

Explain why you think your eating plan is healthy.

____

____

Eat Healthy Challenge

Dear Parents and Guardians,

As part of our class focus on Healthy Habits, we would like families to take part in our Eat Healthy Challenge.

The purpose of the Eat Healthy Challenge is to encourage kids to follow a healthy diet.

Challenge your child to have at least five portions of fruits and vegetables a day. Over the next five days, keep track of the number of fruits and vegetables your child eats.

Every time your child eats a fruit or vegetable, color in a box on the chart. At the end of five days complete the reflection sheet showing how your child did.

In addition, whole families are welcome to take the challenge!

Your family's participation and support are greatly appreciated!

Kind Regards,

____

Recording Chart: Eat Healthy Challenge

Can you eat at least five servings of fruits and vegetables a day for five days in a row?
Good luck on the Eat Healthy Challenge!

Day 1	Day 2	Day 3	Day 4	Day 5

1. **How do you think you did? Explain.**

____

____

Recording Chart: Eat Healthy Challenge (continued)

2. Do you think you made healthy food choices? Explain your thinking.

____

____

3. Who helped to make your food choices?

____

____

4. What was the best part about the challenge?

____

____

5. What was the hardest part about the challenge?

____

____

6. What are your favourite fruits and vegetables?

____

____

Eat Healthy Certificate

Get Enough Sleep

People need sleep to keep healthy, happy, and able to do their best. Sometimes when people don't get enough sleep they feel grumpy and tired. Children ages 5 to 12 need between ten and eleven hours of sleep each night!

Sleep helps your brain, so you can:

- Remember what you learn
- Concentrate and be alert
- Think of new ideas
- Solve problems better

Sleep helps your body, so you can:

- Stay healthy and be able to fight sickness
- Grow strong

Here are some sleep tips for a good night's sleep:

- Make sure your bedroom is cool, dark, and quiet
- Exercise during the day
- Keep a regular bedtime
- Don't drink sodas that have caffeine

Brain Stretch: Get Enough Sleep!

1. Why is sleep important?

____

____

____

____

2. How do you feel if you don't get enough sleep? Explain.

____

____

____

____

Stress Busters

Stress describes a feeling you have when you are worried or uncomfortable about something. Sometimes stress can cause you to have feelings like anger, frustration, or fear. Sometimes stress might be the reason you have a headache or stomachache. Some people who are stressed don't feel like eating or can't sleep. Other people may have trouble concentrating at school or become forgetful.

Here are a few stress buster tips:

- Talk to someone you about how you are feeling
- Take deep breaths and breathe out slowly
- Do some exercise
- Write a journal about how you are feeling and why
- Do a fun activity you enjoy

Brain Stretch: Work with a partner to complete the chart below.

Reasons Kids May Become Stressed	Things They Can Do When That Happens

May I Recommend...

Recommend two things people can do to have a healthy lifestyle. Make sure to explain your thinking!

I recommend...	Draw a picture.

Physical Fitness: Activity Ideas

Activity Idea: Physical Fitness Survey

As a class, make a list of all of the activities that students might do to be physically active. Answers will vary and might include: skipping rope, riding a bike, dancing, taking a walk, etc. Once the list is complete, survey students to see which activities they have tried and put tally marks beside the activities.

Discussion Starters:

- How often do you do an activity?
- What do you like about it? How does it make you feel?
- Where do you go to do these activities?
- What activity is on the list that you haven't tried, but would like to?

Activity Idea: Let's Get Physical!

In a whole-group setting, show students how to check their pulse. Next, have students do a vigorous physical activity, such as jumping jacks, running on the spot, or dancing around the room to upbeat music. Once they have completed the vigorous physical activity, ask students if they feel their heart is beating faster, their lungs are working harder, and/or their bodies feel warm. Explain and reinforce the concept that vigorous physical activity is important to help keep the body healthy and strong.

Discussion Starters:

- Ask students to reflect on the physical activity survey and choose which activities would be labeled as a vigorous physical activity. Encourage students to explain their thinking.
- Ask students how the vigorous physical activity made them feel.

Activity Idea: Physical Activity Challenge

Encourage students to keep physically active every day. Ask students to take part in the five-day Physical Activity Challenge. Each day, students will record the physical activities they did, along with the amount of time they did them. Challenge students to do at least 30 minutes of physical activity a day.

As a whole group, brainstorm a list of physical activities they could do. Some examples are:

- playing tag
- playing sports
- dancing
- skipping rope
- hopscotch
- swimming
- aerobics
- hiking
- riding a bike
- weight training
- walking/jogging

Other Extension Activities:

- Have students use the word search black line master to create their own word search of physical activities.
- Have students conduct surveys about favorite physical activities.
- Have students create an aerobics routine to an upbeat song. Students can take turns leading the class in aerobics activities.
- Have students write a biography of a sports personality. Make sure students include their reasons for choosing that person and what characteristics that person has to have done so well in their chosen sport.

Physical Fitness: Journal Topics

1. How do you feel about gym class?

2. Do you think students should have 30 minutes of exercise at school a day? Explain.

3. You want to play a particular sport, but don't think you are good enough. What should you do?

4. Some members of your family are out of shape. What could you do to encourage them to get in shape?

5. How is being physically active an important part of healthy living?

6. If you get tired before the rest of the class does during gym, what can you do about it?

7. What is your favorite sport? Give your reasons.

8. If you could win an Olympic gold medal in any sport, which sport would you choose? Explain.

9. Sports are not the only way to be physically active. What are some other things you can do to be physically active?

10. Are you more physically active on weekdays or on the weekends? Explain.

Physical Fitness Survey

Complete the survey to learn more about your fitness habits.

	Questions	Rarely	Often	Always
1.	What types of physical activities do you do outside school?			
2.	Do you participate in an organized physical activity at least once a week?			
3.	Are you involved in at least one extra-curricular physical activity in school?			
4.	Do you participate in active activities (such as basketball, skipping, tag, etc.) during recess?			
5.	Do you and your family do physical activities together?			
6.	Do you walk or ride your bike to and from school?			
7.	Do you have fun when you are participating in physical activities?			
8.	Do you participate in any team sports?			
9.	Would you rather be active than play on the computer or watch TV?			

Look over your responses. Which response did you have most often?

____

What do you think this fitness survey reveals about your fitness level? Explain.

____

____

____

____

Recording Chart: Physical Activity Challenge

Congratulations for taking part in the Physical Activity Challenge!

For the next five days, keep track of all the kinds of physical activity you do. Make sure you include things like walking to school, dancing, skipping rope, playing team sports, riding your bike, or playing outside with your friends. Can you do at least 30 minutes of physical activity a day?

	What kind of physical activity did you do?	How many minutes?
Day 1		
Day 2		
Day 3		
Day 4		
Day 5		

Think About It: Physical Activity Challenge

1. How do you think you did?

____

____

2. What do you enjoy about doing physical activities? Explain.

____

____

3. What do you not enjoy about doing physical activities? Explain.

____

____

4. If you could become an expert in two sports, which would you choose?

____

____

5. List the physical activities you would like to try.

____

____

____

CONGRATULATIONS!

Name: _______________________

YOU HAVE COMPLETED THE PHYSICAL ACTIVITY CHALLENGE

Conflict Resolution: Activity Ideas

Activity Idea: What Is Conflict Resolution?

Introduce the idea of conflict resolution to students. Conflict resolution is a process to help solve problems in a positive way. Each person involved is encouraged to take responsibility for their actions. Clear steps for conflict resolution might include:

- Finding out what the problem is
- Listening without interrupting
- Talking it out
- Coming up with different solutions

Discuss and review the above process with students. Role-play different situations so students can practice walking through the process. Students should be encouraged to try and understand the other person's perspective. The teacher may wish to use situations that are reflected in their class. Encourage students to come up with different solutions so they get in the habit of looking for another solution if the first one does not work. In addition, post the steps for conflict resolution on the board for easy student reference.

Activity Idea: When People Feel Angry...

Explain to students that sometimes people can feel angry about a situation. People might feel angry because:

- Something is unfair
- Something has been taken away from them
- Something has been broken
- Someone was mean or teased them
- Someone is not sharing
- Someone is in their space

Ask students to remember a time when they felt angry. Have students explain what happened and how they handled the situation. Discuss what would be the best way to handle different situations.

Activity Idea: Acts of Kindness

Brainstorm with students what it means to be kind. Record their responses on chart paper. Next, go through the student-generated list and have students name the feelings they associate with each act of kindness.

Discussion Starters:

- What are some ways you can be kind to others?
- How does it feel to be kind? How does it feel to be mean?

Next, have students create coupons to give out to people they would like to perform an act of kindness for. Coupons could be for another student, a family member, neighbor, teacher, etc.

Activity Idea: Bullying

Help students gain a clear understanding of bullying. Bullying can be described as the act of hurting someone physically or psychologically on purpose. Students should also be made aware that bullies come in all shapes and sizes. Usually someone is bullied repeatedly. Some forms of bullying include:

Physical: hitting, punching, tripping, shoving, stealing belongings, locking someone in or out, etc.

Verbal: teasing, putting someone down, taunting, making embarrassing remarks, etc.

Relational: excluding someone from a group, spreading rumors, ignoring someone, ostracizing someone, etc.

It is hoped that if students can understand what a person feels like when bullied, students will develop empathy and help stop bullying.

Dealing with Conflicts

Think of a conflict you have had recently with a friend or family member.

1. **Describe the conflict.**

____

____

____

____

2. **How did you solve this conflict?**

____

____

____

____

3. **If you think there was a better way to solve this conflict, explain what the better way is.**

____

____

____

4. **If you think this was the best way to solve this conflict, explain why you feel that wa**

____

____

____

Let's solve the problem!

Step 1
What is
the
problem?

Step 2
Listen without interrupting.
Step 3
Talk it out.

Step 4

Come up with a solution.

Step 5

Remember to put yourself in the other person's shoes.

Acts of Kindness

Acts of kindness let people know that you care about them. Color the boxes green that are examples of acts of kindness.

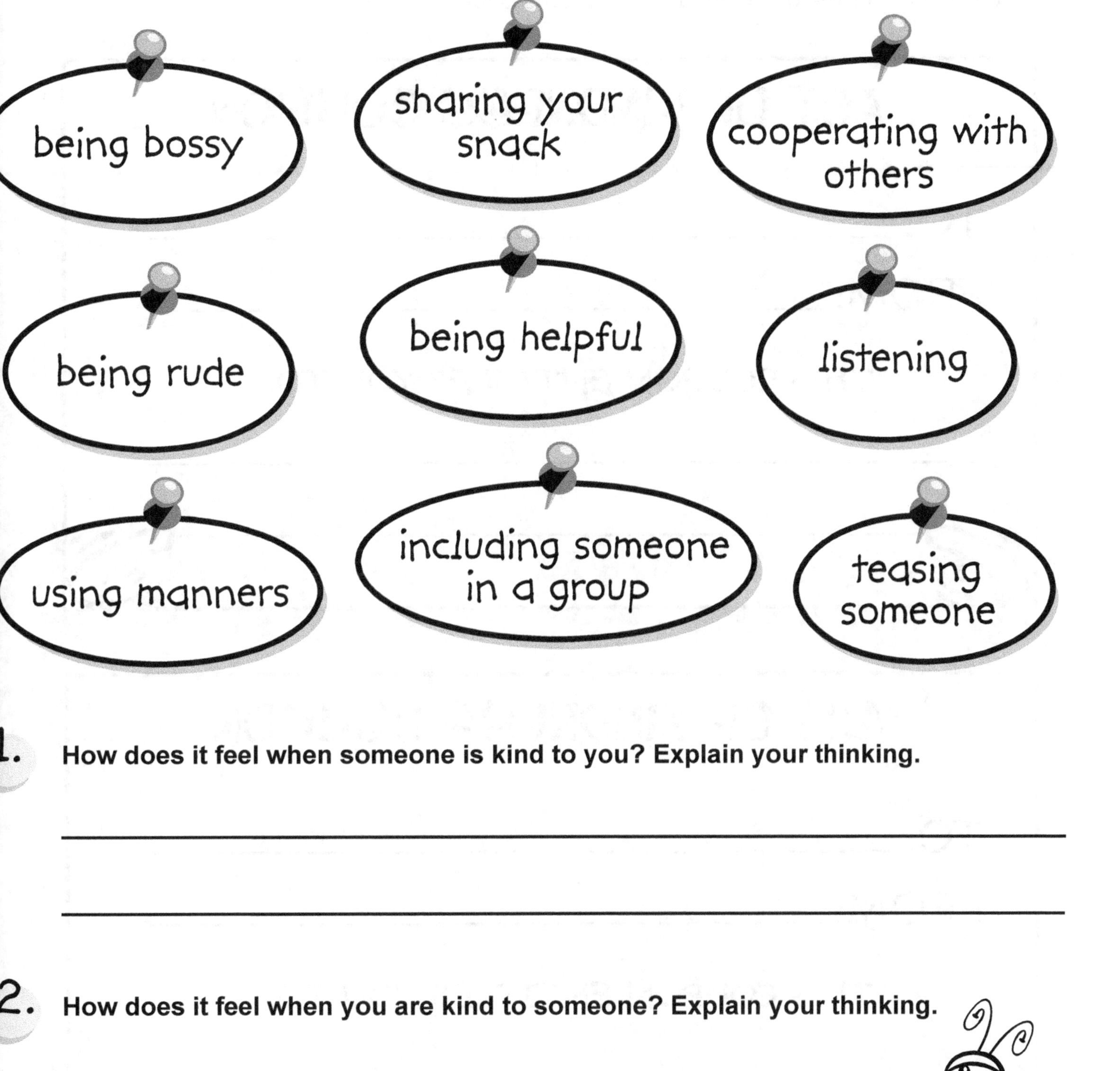

1. How does it feel when someone is kind to you? Explain your thinking.

____

____

2. How does it feel when you are kind to someone? Explain your thinking.

____

____

Act of Kindness Coupons

Create your own Act of Kindness coupon. Give out these coupons to the people in your life whom you would like to perform an act of kindness for.

ACT OF KINDNESS COUPON

TO: _______________________________________

FROM: _____________________________________

THIS COUPON ENTITLES YOU TO:

____

ACT OF KINDNESS COUPON

TO: _______________________________________

FROM: _____________________________________

THIS COUPON ENTITLES YOU TO:

____

Stop Bullying: Journal Topics

What is bullying?

Do you think there are more bullies or victims in your school? Explain your thinking.

Do you think bullying is a serious problem in your school? Explain why or why not.

Do you think it helps to tell an adult about bullying? Explain why or why not.

Do you think it is possible to make a bully understand how they make their victim feel? Explain your thinking.

Have you ever witnessed anyone being bullied? What happened?

Do you think that you have ever bullied anyone? If so, what happened?

Why do you think someone becomes a bully?

What can each of you do to help stop bullying? Give details.

Bullying: What Should You Do?

1. How do you think a person being bullied feels?

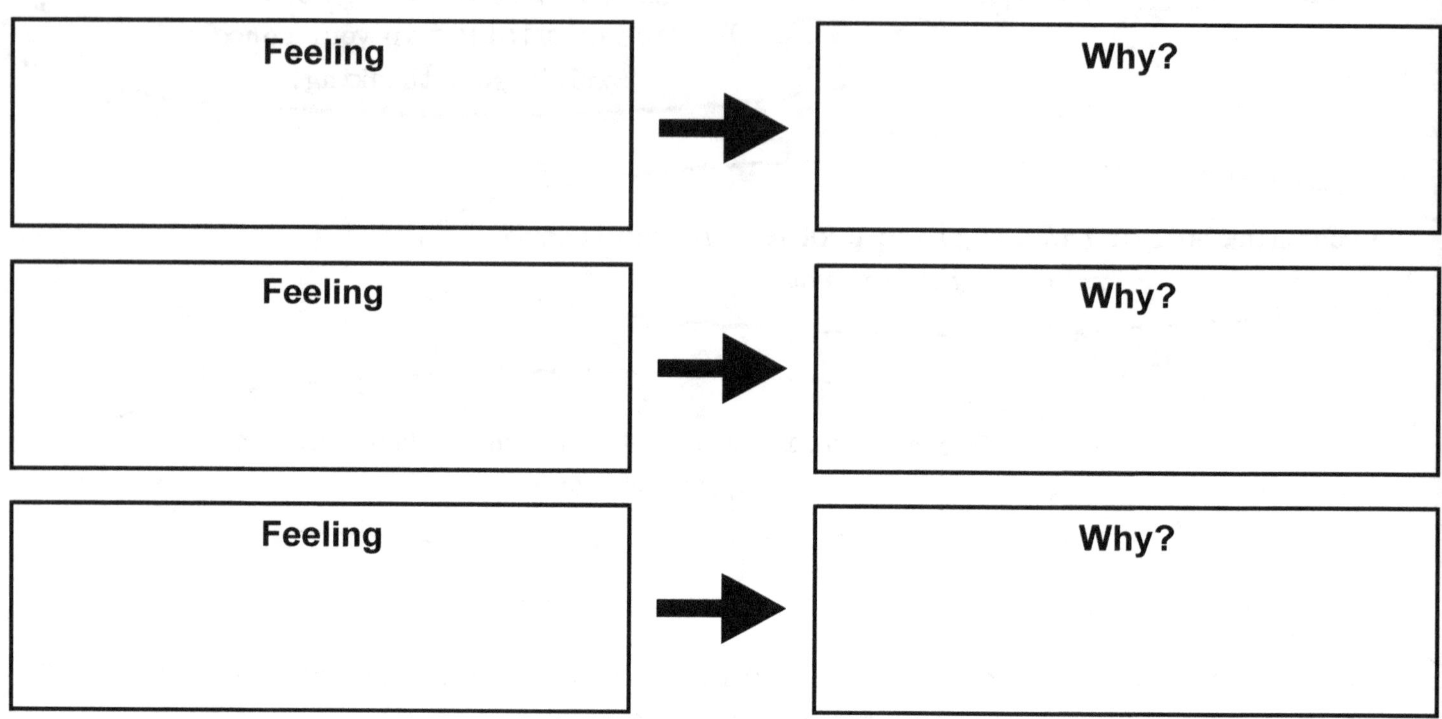

2. Circle in **green** the things you should do when bullied.
Circle in **red** the things you should not do when bullied.

Stop Bullying!

What is bullying?

Bullying is when someone mistreats someone on purpose, as in:

- name-calling or using put-downs
- using physical violence
- ignoring or excluding
- spreading rumors

1. What are three things a person who is being bullied can do?

a. ____

b. ____

c. ____

2. What are three things you can do if you see someone else being bullied?

a. ____

b. ____

c. ____

Bullying Scenarios: What Could You Do?

With a partner, discuss and write a suggestion about what to do for each scenario below from the perspective of: someone who is a bystander and someone who is being bullied.

Examples of bullying:	What could a bystander do?	What could the person being bullied do?
Bumping into someone in the hall on purpose		
Calling someone names		
Sending someone nasty emails		
Threatening to beat up someone if they don't do what you want		
Making someone give you money		
Not letting someone sit next to you even though there is enough room		
Spreading rumors about someone		

A Letter of Advice

Choose:

- Write a letter of advice to someone who is being bullied.
- Write a letter of advice to someone who is being a bully.

Dear _________________________________ ,

Your friend,

____

Personal Safety: Activity Tips

Activity Idea: Role-Playing

Have students work in pairs or in small groups and act out different safety scenarios to show what they would do. Scenarios might include:

- A stranger approaches you
- A cyber pal wants to meet you in person
- A friend dares you cross into an area that says No Trespassing

Activity Idea: Safety Tip Poster

Have students create posters to promote safety tips for various situations and places. Topics may include personal safety, cyber safety, safety in public places, or safety tips for certain activities, such as swimming or riding a bicycle. Make sure to go to the website BAM! Body and Mind for an excellent source of safety information in kid-friendly language. Download safety information cards for student use.

https://www.cdc.gov/bam/index.html

Activity Idea: Create a Safety Brochure

Have students create a safety brochure. This project could be done in small groups or individually. Headings for the brochure could include:

- What to Do in an Emergency
- Home Safety
- Public Places: Safety Tips
- Swimming Safety Tips
- Internet Safety Tips

1. Demonstrate for students how to fold a large piece of paper the same way the brochure will be folded.
2. Next, show students how to plan the layout using a pencil.
   - Write the heading for each section where it should be in the brochure
   - Leave room underneath each section to write information
   - Leave room for graphics or pictures
3. Students can then write information to fit the headings.
4. Encourage students to add eye-catching pictures or graphics and slogans.

Internet Safety Tips

Keep in mind the following Internet safety tips when you're using your computer at home or at school:

1. Never give out any personal information, such as your name, age, address, or school.

2. Never send a cyber pal a picture of yourself without checking with your parent or guardian.

3. Never respond to messages on a bulletin board that make you feel uncomfortable.

4. Never arrange a face-to-face meeting with a cyber pal without checking with your parent or guardian.

5. Be aware that people online might not be who they say they are.

6. Never set up a "user" profile to keep your personal information safe.

7. Never give out your password!

Brain Stretch:

1. Do you practice these Internet safety tips? Why or why not?

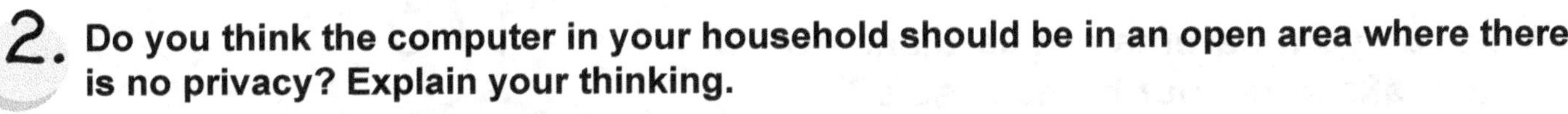

____

____

2. Do you think the computer in your household should be in an open area where there is no privacy? Explain your thinking.

____

____

3. Should your parent or guardian have access to your email account? Explain your thinking.

____

____

Personal Safety: Journal Topics

1. Whom could you turn to in an emergency?

2. Describe some situations that young people get into that threaten their personal safety.

3. What would you do if there was a fire in your house?

4. What responsibilities are involved when baby-sitting or taking care of young children?

5. Why do you think it is important to practice Internet safety?

6. How do you know whether you can trust someone? By the way they look? The job they do?

7. What do your parents or guardians do to make sure your home is safe?

Analyzing Advertisements

Cut out and paste in the space below an advertisement from a magazine or newspaper and answer the questions below.

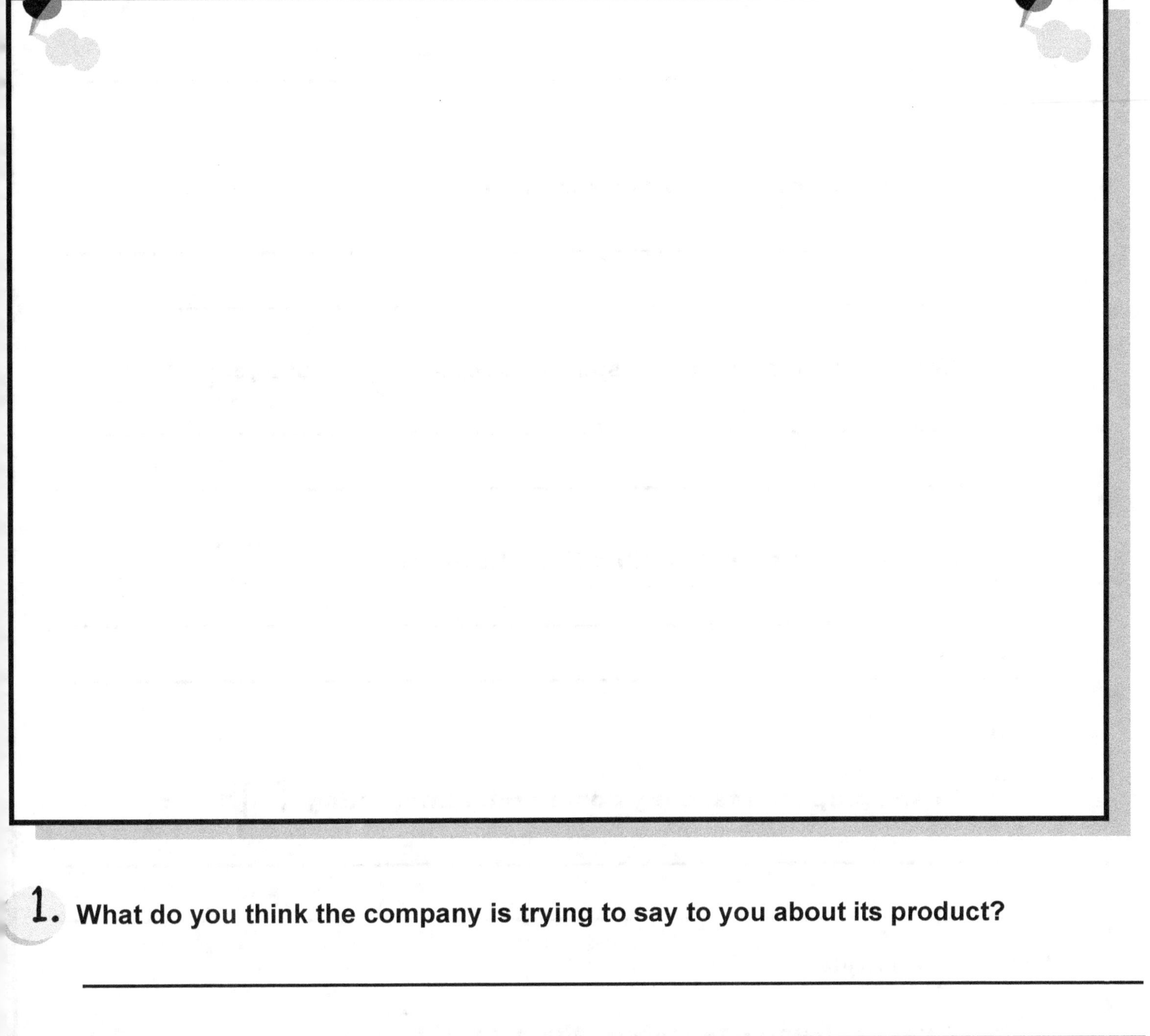

1. What do you think the company is trying to say to you about its product?

____

____

2. Do you agree or disagree with that message? Why, or why not?

____

____

Commercial Checklist

Write a radio or TV anti-smoking or anti-drug commercial.

My commercial is about ___________________________________

a. My commercial tells a clear message. ☐

____

____

b. My commercial gives reasons to support my message. ☐

____

____

c. My commercial ends with a thought to remember. ☐

____

____

Props:

d. I used props to make my commercial interesting. ☐

____

____

Performance Style:

e. I practiced and used interesting words. ☐

____

____

Anti-________________ T-shirt

Design a T-shirt that encourages people to stop smoking or to stay away from drugs.

How Do These Factors Affect You?

Think about smoking, drinking, and drugs. What influences have your friends, family, the media, and teachers had on you as you develop attitudes about these things? Complete the chart by describing how you have been influenced in either a positive or negative manner.

FACTOR	ILLEGAL DRUGS	ALCOHOL	CIGARETTES
1. FAMILY			
2. FRIENDS			
3. CELEBRITIES			

How Do These Factors Affect You? (continued)

Think about smoking, drinking, and drugs. What influences have your friends, family, the media, and teachers had on you as you develop attitudes about these things? Complete the chart by describing how you have been influenced in either a positive or negative manner.

FACTOR	ILLEGAL DRUGS	ALCOHOL	CIGARETTES
4. MEDIA			
5. TEACHERS			

Who or what do you think has influenced you most? Explain.

What I Think I Know. What I Wonder About.

Write or draw in the space below.

Reporting Ideas

Non-Fiction Reports

Encourage students to read informational text and to recall in their own words what they have read. Provide a theme-related space or table and subject-related materials and artifacts such as books, tapes, posters, magazines, etc.

Have students explore the different sections usually found in a non-fiction book:

1. Title Page: The book title and the author's name

2. Table of Contents: The title of each chapter, what page it starts on, and where you can find specific information

3. Glossary: The meaning of special words used in the book

4. Index: The ABC list of specific topics you can find in the book

Next, discuss criteria of a good research project. They should include:

- A presentation board or other medium

- Proper grammar and punctuation, for example, capitals and periods

- Print size that can be read from far away

- Neat coloring and detailed drawings

Oral Reports

Encourage students to talk about what they have learned and to make a presentation to the class. Here are tips to discuss with students:

- Use your best voice, speak slowly, and make sure your voice is loud so everyone can hear

- Look at your audience and try not to sway

- Introduce your topic in an interesting way, for instance, by using a riddle or a question

- Choose the most important information to tell

- Point to pictures, a model, or a diorama as you present

A Web About...

Fill in the circles below.

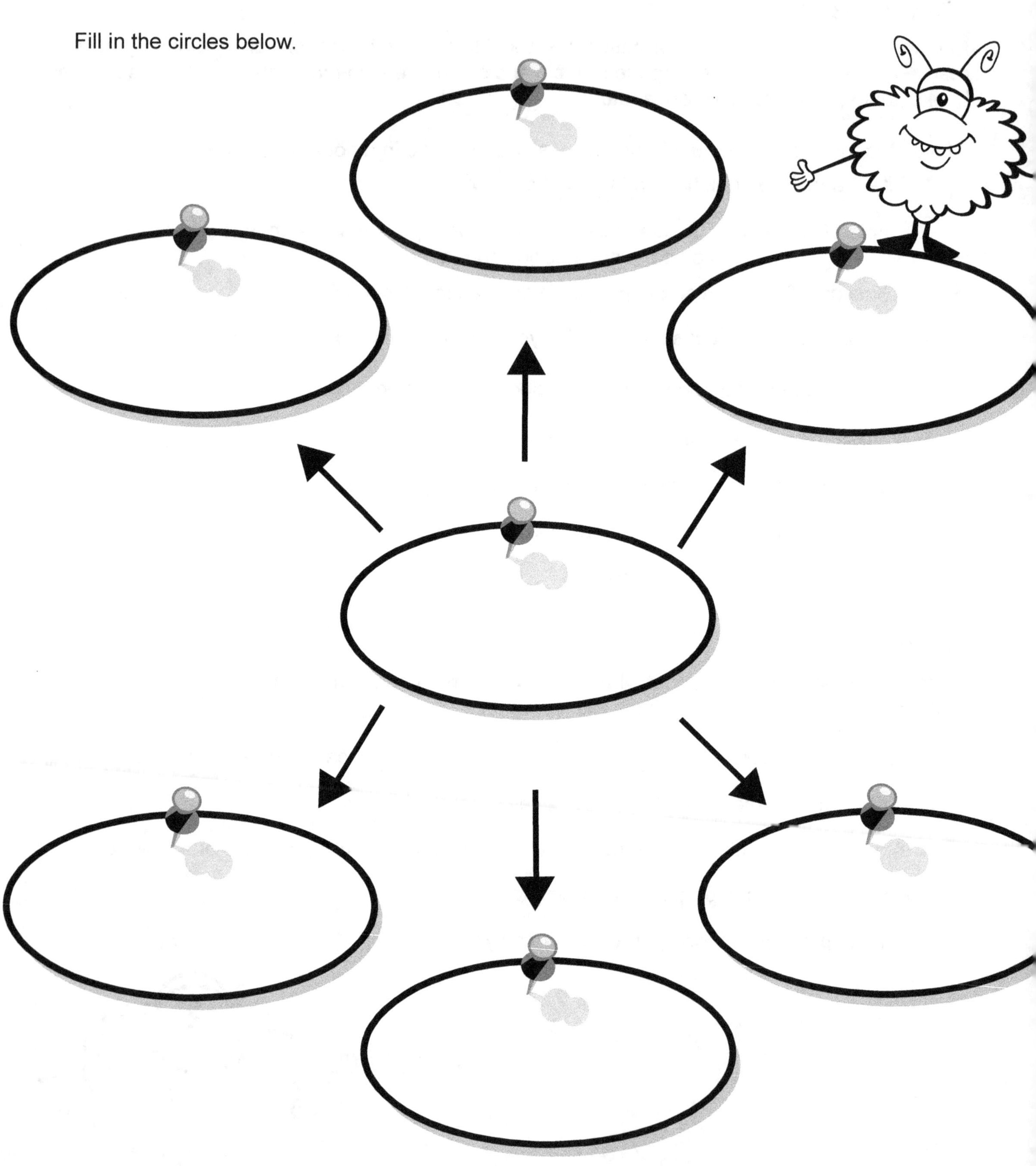

A T-chart About...

Fill in the chart below.

A Venn Diagram About...

Fill in the diagram below.

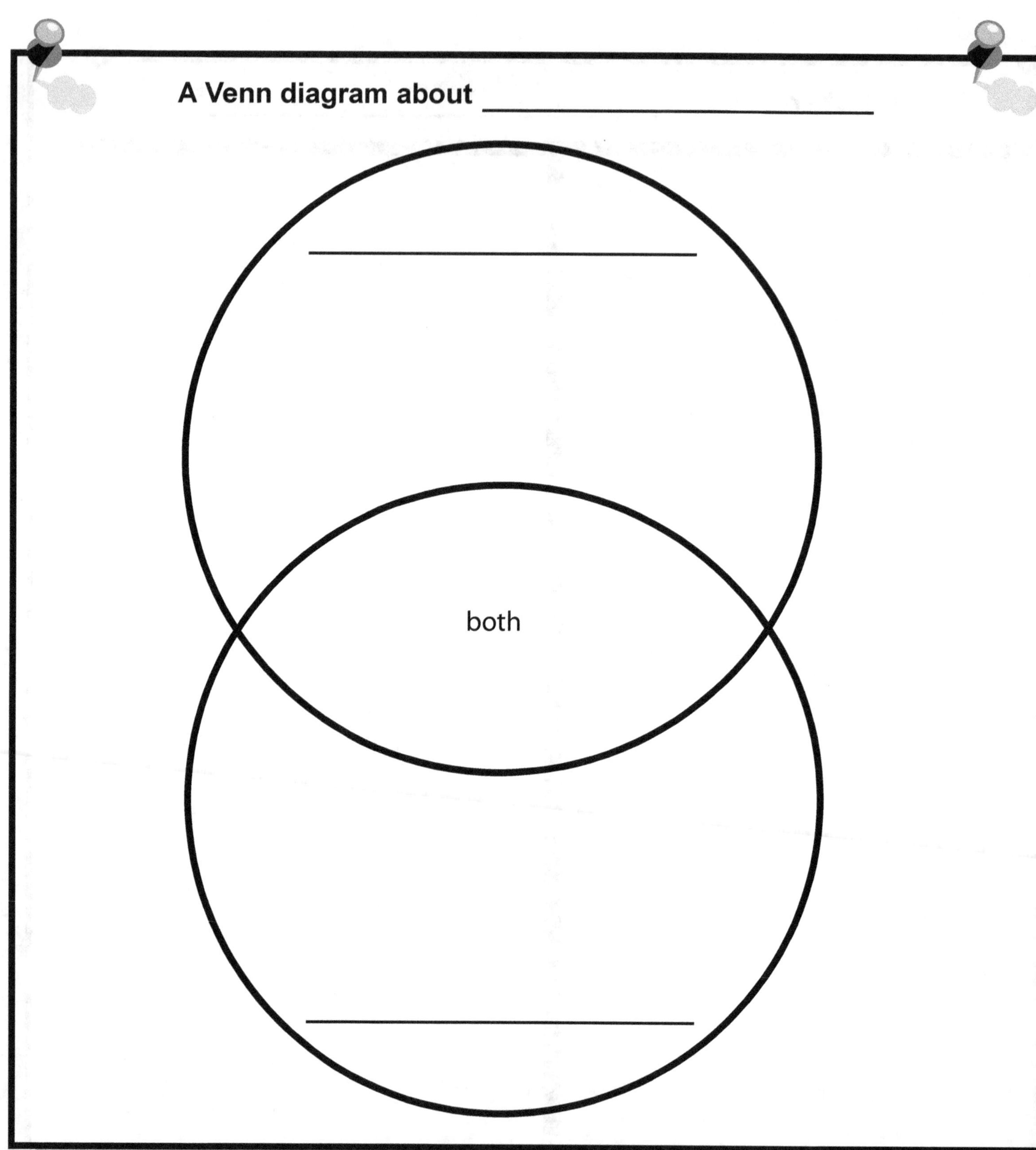

Write a Letter

I am writing a letter to ____

because ____

Dear ____ ,

Your friend,

____

Conduct a Survey on a Health-Related Issue.

Survey outline:

1. What is the question? ____ .

2. How many people are you going to ask? _______________________________ .

Answer Choices	Tally Marks

3. Once you have completed your survey, create a bar graph to show the information.

Health Survey Results

Conduct a survey.

1. I conducted a survey about ____ .

2. I asked this question because ____

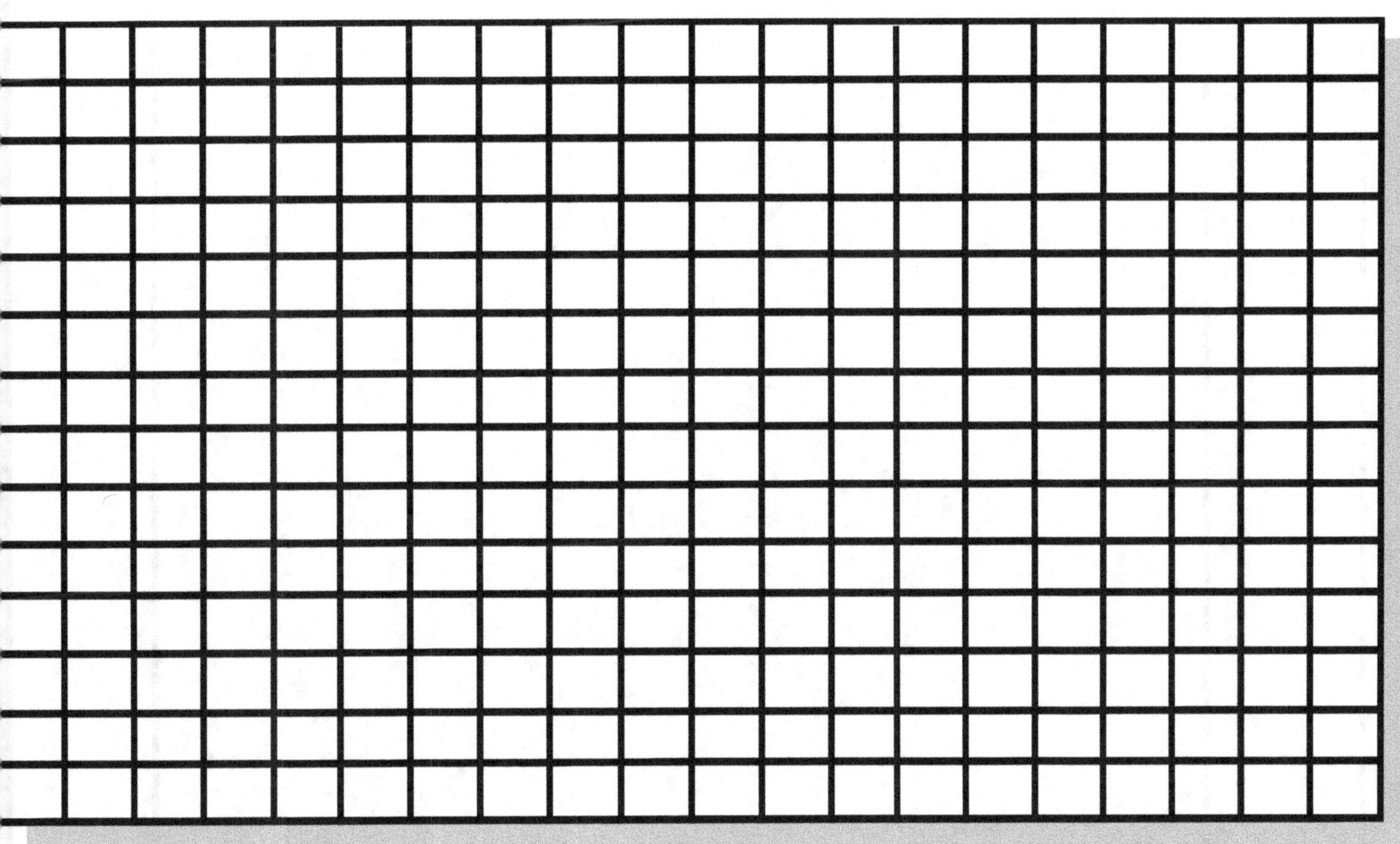

3. From the results of the survey I learned that ...

____

____

____

____

My Own Health Word Search

Create a word search and share it with your classmates.

Word Search Title: _______________________________

Word List

-
-
-
-
-

-
-
-
-
-

-
-
-
-
-

Magazine Checklist

You have been selected to create a new kids' health magazine. Here is a checklist for a top-quality magazine:

Magazine Title: ____

Magazine Cover:

- ☐ **The title of the magazine is easy to read and prominent on the cover.**

- ☐ **There is an attractive illustration to let readers know the theme of the magazine.**

- ☐ **There are one or two highlight statements about what is inside the magazine.**

Editor's Page:

- ☐ **The letter is addressed to the readers.**

- ☐ **The letter lets readers know why you think it is important to have a healthy lifestyle.**

Table of Contents:

- ☐ **There is a complete listing of what is in the magazine.**

Advertisements:

- ☐ **There are student-created advertisements for healthy products throughout the magazine.**

Magazine Plan:

- ☐ **All the jobs on the magazine plan are complete.**

Some article ideas and other columns to include in your magazine:

• Healthy Eating	• Bullying	• Substance Abuse
• Sports Tips	• Biography of someone you admire	• Fitness
• Survey Results	• Peer Pressure	• Internet Safety
• Importance of Sleeping	• Eating Disorders	• Recipes

Magazine Production Plan

Group members: ____

Use the magazine plan to assign jobs for each group member.

Job	Group Member	Complete

Write a Magazine Article

Pretend you are a reporter for Kids Now! Health Magazine. Write an article to help kids understand the importance and benefits of a healthy lifestyle. Some ideas you may wish to write about include:

- Personal Safety Tips
- Importance of Eating a Balanced Diet
- Internet Safety

These are the parts of an article you need to include:

1. The **HEADLINE** names the article.
2. The **BYLINE** shows the name of the author. (You)
3. The **BEGINNING** gives the most important idea.
4. The **MIDDLE** gives supporting details about the idea.
5. The **ENDING** usually gives the reader an idea to remember.

Article Checklist:

Content:

☐ I have a **HEADLINE** that names the article.

☐ I have a **BYLINE** that shows my name as the author.

☐ I have a **BEGINNING** that gives the most important facts.

☐ I have a **MIDDLE** that gives details about the article.

☐ I have an **ENDING** that gives the reader an idea to remember.

Grammar and Style:

☐ I used my neatest printing and included a clear title.

☐ I included a colorful picture.

☐ I spelled my words correctly.

☐ I used interesting words.

☐ I checked for capitals, periods, commas, and question marks.

Health Issues: Taking One Point of View

Write an article that gives one point of view about a health issue. Use the outline to plan your article. Some ideas you may want to write about are:

- Should students have 30 minutes mandatory exercise every day?
- Should smoking be banned?
- Should candy and soft drinks be banned from schools?

A Statement of Your Point of View

____

Assertion	**Supporting Evidence**
Assertion	**Supporting Evidence**
Assertion	**Supporting Evidence**

An Advertisement for ______________________

Create an advertisement for a health product or service.

Magazine Rubric

1. Group Members: ____

____

2. Project: ____

Criteria	Level 1	Level 2	Level 3	Level 4
Content/Information • information • accuracy • supporting details	- limited information - few supporting details	- some of the required information - some supporting details	- most of the required information - accurate and complete supporting details	- comprehensive information - very thorough supporting details
Writing Conventions • spelling • grammar • punctuation	- spelling and grammar errors in good copy - inconsistent punctuation	- some spelling, grammar, and punctuation errors in good copy	- most of the spelling, grammar, and punctuation is correct in good copy	- all spelling, grammar, and punctuation are correct in good copy
Graphics / Pictures • match information • colour enhanced	- pictures rarely match information - incomplete	- pictures partially match information - some pictures are incomplete	- pictures are complete and appropriate	- pictures are outstanding and consistently match information
Overall Presentation • neatness • organization	- little organization or neatness	- some organization and neatness	- general organization and neatness	- outstanding organization and neatness

3. Teacher Comments: _______________________________________

____

____

Student Rubric

Level	Student Participation Descriptor
Level 4	Student consistently contributes to class discussions and activities by offering ideas and asking questions.
Level 3	Student usually contributes to class discussions and activities by offering ideas and asking questions.
Level 2	Student sometimes contributes to class discussions and activities by offering ideas and asking questions.
Level 1	Student rarely contributes to class discussions or activities by offering ideas or asking questions.

Level	Understanding of Concepts Descriptor
Level 4	Student shows a thorough understanding of all or almost all concepts and consistently gives appropriate and complete explanations independently. No teacher support is needed.
Level 3	Student shows a good understanding of most concepts and usually gives complete or nearly complete explanations. Infrequent teacher support is needed.
Level 2	Student shows a satisfactory understanding of most concepts and sometimes gives appropriate, but incomplete, explanations. Teacher support is sometimes needed.
Level 1	Student shows little understanding of concepts and rarely gives complete explanations. Intensive teacher support is needed.

Level	Communication of Concepts Descriptor
Level 4	Student consistently communicates with clarity and precision in written and oral work. Student consistently uses appropriate terminology and vocabulary.
Level 3	Student usually communicates with clarity and precision in written and oral work. Student usually uses appropriate terminology and vocabulary.
Level 2	Student sometimes communicates with clarity and precision in written and oral work. Student sometimes uses appropriate terminology and vocabulary.
Level 1	Student rarely communicates with clarity or precision in written or oral work.

Class Evaluation List

Fill in the following:

Student Name	Class Participation	Understanding of Concepts	Communication of Concepts	Overall Evaluation

Physical Activity Rubric

	Level 1	Level 2	Level 3	Level 4
Understanding of Physical Activity Concepts	Student demonstrates a limited understanding of concepts.	Student demonstrates a satisfactory understanding of concepts.	Student demonstrates a complete understanding of concepts.	Student demonstrates a thorough understanding of concepts.
Application of Skills Taught	Student applies few of the required skills.	Student applies some of the required skills.	Student applies most of the required skills.	Student applies almost all of the required skills.
Participation	Constant teacher encouragement is needed.	Some teacher encouragement is needed.	Little teacher encouragement is needed.	Student almost always participates without teacher encouragement.
Sportsmanship	Student needs encouragement to be a team player.	Student will occasionally share, help, and encourage others.	Student will usually share, help, and encourage others.	Student acts as a team leader. Student will consistently share, help, and encourage others.
Safety	Student requires constant reminders regarding safety or the safe use of equipment and facilities.	Student requires occasional reminders regarding safety or the safe use of equipment and facilities.	Student requires few reminders regarding safety or the safe use of equipment and facilities.	Student requires almost no reminders regarding safety or the safe use of equipment and facilities.

Thinking About My Work

Thinking About My Work

1. I am proud of:

    ____

2. I want to learn more about:

    ____

3. I need to work on:

    ____

4. I will do better by:

    ____

Thinking About My Work

1. I am proud of:

    ____

2. I want to learn more about:

    ____

3. I need to work on:

    ____

4. I will do better by:

    ____

Useful Health Websites

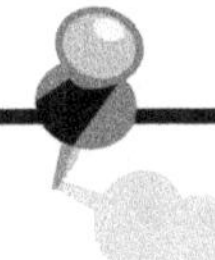

1. All About Kids' Health
http://kidshealth.org/en/kids/

2. Safe Kids Worldwide
https://www.safekids.org/united-states-0

3. An Anti-Bullying Site
https://www.stopbullying.gov/

4. Stay Alert …Stay Safe
http://kidshealth.org/en/kids/watch/

5. The American Lung Association
http://www.lung.org/

6. The American Dental Association
http://www.mouthhealthykids.org/en

7. Kids Environment, Kids Health
https://kids.niehs.nih.gov/

8. MyPlate Food Guide
http://kidshealth.org/en/kids/pyramid.html

9. Fire Safety Tips for Kids
http://www.firesafetyforkids.org/fire-safety-rules.html

10. Websites for Kids and Teens
https://www.cdc.gov/family/kidsites/index.htm

11. Girls' Health
https://www.girlshealth.gov/

CONGRATULATIONS!
Name:
you are a health expert!
GREAT work!